An Affirmation Journal for Mind, Body, and Soul.

Author:

CR Hendrix

This Journal Belongs to

____

Author Foreword:

I hope these affirmations help you in the same way they've helped me. You deserve to live a life that you enjoy, a life that you're proud of, and a life on your terms. May these affirmations take you on a journey to your highest self. I am rooting for you today and everyday! With love and gratitude, CR!

Empower

"We do not need magic to transform our world. We carry all of the power we need inside ourselves already."

-J.K. Rowling

I am prepared.
I am equipped.
Everything I need is
within me.

Date ____________________

Morning ○ Afternoon ○ Evening ○

I am prepared.
I am equipped.
Everything I need is within me.

Write and repeat todays affirmation three times:

1. ______________________________
2. ______________________________
3. ______________________________

What does this affirmation mean to you?

____

____

____

____

____

____

____

____

____

____

Take a moment for introspection.
Write down the intangible
things you are equipped with.

I honor the path that I am on. I work to be better on this path.

Date________________

Morning ○ Afternoon ○ Evening ○

I honor the path that I am on.
I work to be better on
this path.

Write and repeat todays affirmation three times:

1. ____

2. ____

3. ____

What does this affirmation mean to you?

____

____

____

____

____

____

____

____

____

____

Take a deep breath.
Reflect on your current path.
Write down 3 ways you wish to be better.

Everything happens
for me not
to me.

Date___________________

Morning ○ Afternoon ○ Evening ○

Everything happens for me not to me.

Write and repeat todays affirmation three times:

1. ______________________________
2. ______________________________
3. ______________________________

What does this affirmation mean to you?

____

____

____

____

____

____

____

____

____

____

Reminisce on all the things that are happening for you. Write down all the things that are happening for you.

If it can be done.
I can do it.
Nothing is beyond
my reach.

Date________________

Morning ○ Afternoon ○ Evening ○

If it can be done.
I can do it.
Nothing is beyond my reach.

Write and repeat todays affirmation three times:

1. ______________________________
2. ______________________________
3. ______________________________

What does this affirmation mean to you?

____

____

____

____

____

____

____

____

____

____

What is something you've been avoiding?
How are you going to get it done?

I'm in harmony with my spirit. I'm prepared to be myself and only myself.

Date ____________________

Morning ○ Afternoon ○ Evening ○

I'm in harmony with my spirit.
I'm prepared to be myself
and only myself.

Write and repeat todays affirmation three times:

1. ______________________________

2. ______________________________

3. ______________________________

What does this affirmation mean to you?

____

____

____

____

____

____

____

____

____

____

What is your spirit telling you? Write down one thing you will try this week to honor your spirit.

My mouth reflects
what I expect.

Date_______________

Morning ○ Afternoon ○ Evening ○

My mouth reflects
what I expect.

Write and repeat todays affirmation three times:

1. ______________________________
2. ______________________________
3. ______________________________

What does this affirmation mean to you?

____

____

____

____

____

____

____

____

____

____

What are the words you're currently speaking over your life? Write down 3 words you spoke over your life today.

Do those words reflect the life you desire? Write down three more words you will intentionally speak over your life this week.

What's for me
won't pass me by.

Date________________

Morning ○ Afternoon ○ Evening ○

What's for me
won't pass me by.

Write and repeat todays affirmation three times:

1. ____________________
2. ____________________
3. ____________________

What does this affirmation mean to you?

____
____
____
____
____
____
____
____
____
____

Think about your life.
What are some things you thought passed you by? Write them down.
P.S. Nothing and No one can pass you by.

I live a life filled with abundance and endless opportunities.

Date________________

Morning ○ Afternoon ○ Evening ○

I live a life filled with abundance and endless opportunities.

Write and repeat todays affirmation three times:

1. ______________________________
2. ______________________________
3. ______________________________

What does this affirmation mean to you?

____

____

____

____

____

____

____

____

____

____

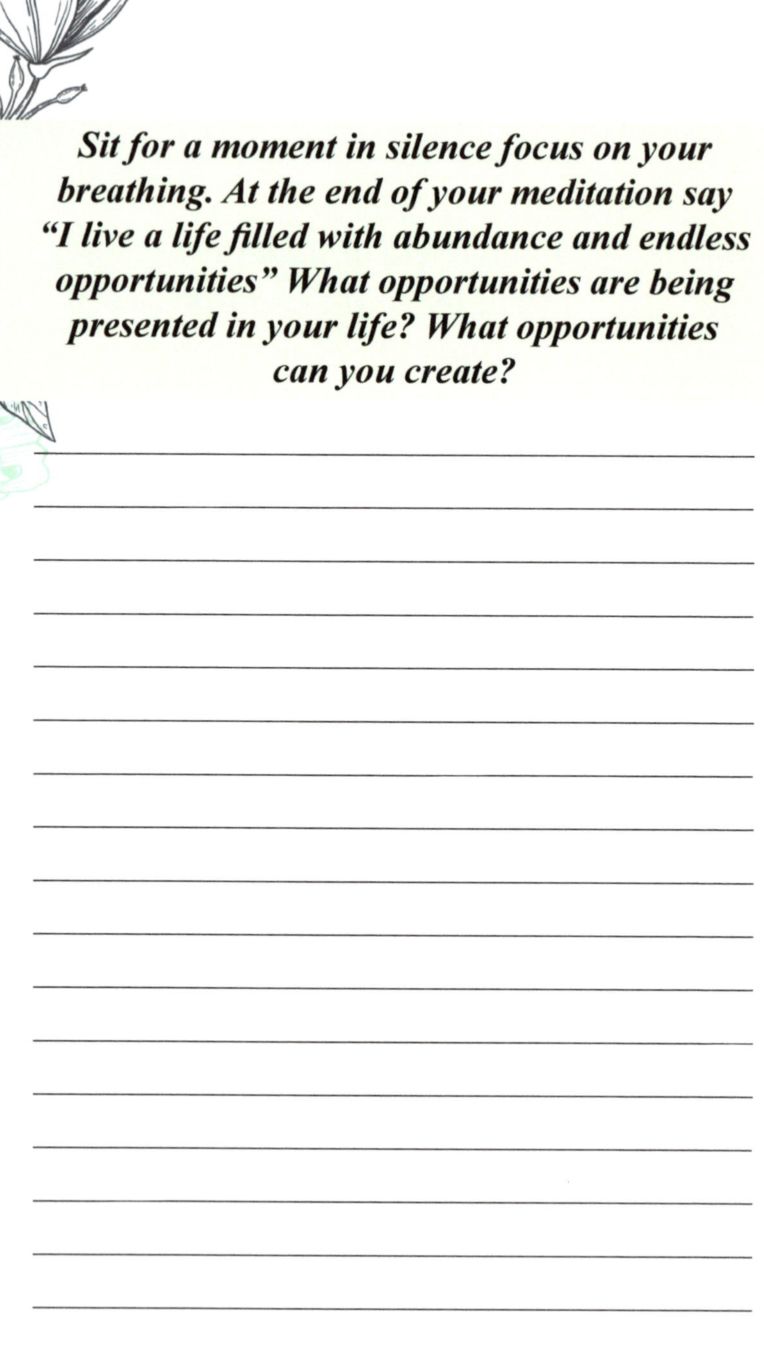

Sit for a moment in silence focus on your breathing. At the end of your meditation say "I live a life filled with abundance and endless opportunities" What opportunities are being presented in your life? What opportunities can you create?

Love

"One of the best guides to how to be self-loving is to give ourselves the love we are often dreaming about receiving from others."
Bell Hooks

I am love.
Wherever I am
love will be.

Date ____________

Morning ○ Afternoon ○ Evening ○

I am love.
Wherever I am
love will be.

Write and repeat todays affirmation three times:

1. ______________________________
2. ______________________________
3. ______________________________

What does this affirmation mean to you?

Take a moment to write a love letter to yourself.

I love who I am.
I love whose I am.

Date________________

Morning ○ Afternoon ○ Evening ○

I love who I am.
I love whose I am.

Write and repeat todays affirmation three times:

1. ________________

2. ________________

3. ________________

What does this affirmation mean to you?

Write down 5 things you love about yourself.

I love my body.
My body loves me.

Date ____________

Morning ○ Afternoon ○ Evening ○

I love my body.
My body loves me.

Write and repeat todays affirmation three times:

1. ______________________________
2. ______________________________
3. ______________________________

What does this affirmation mean to you?

What do you love about your body?
How does your body show you love?

I do not have to prove my worth. I am fearfully and wonderfully made.

Date ____________________

Morning ○ Afternoon ○ Evening ○

I do not have to prove my worth. I am fearfully and wonderfully made.

Write and repeat todays affirmation three times:

1. ____________________
2. ____________________
3. ____________________

What does this affirmation mean to you?

____

____

____

____

____

____

____

____

____

____

Make a list of all the wonderful things you are made of.

I am enough as I was.
I am enough as I am.
I am enough for who
I am becoming.

Date ____________________

Morning ○ Afternoon ○ Evening ○

I am enough as I was.
I am enough as I am.
I am enough for who I am becoming.

Write and repeat todays affirmation three times:

1. ______________________________

2. ______________________________

3. ______________________________

What does this affirmation mean to you?

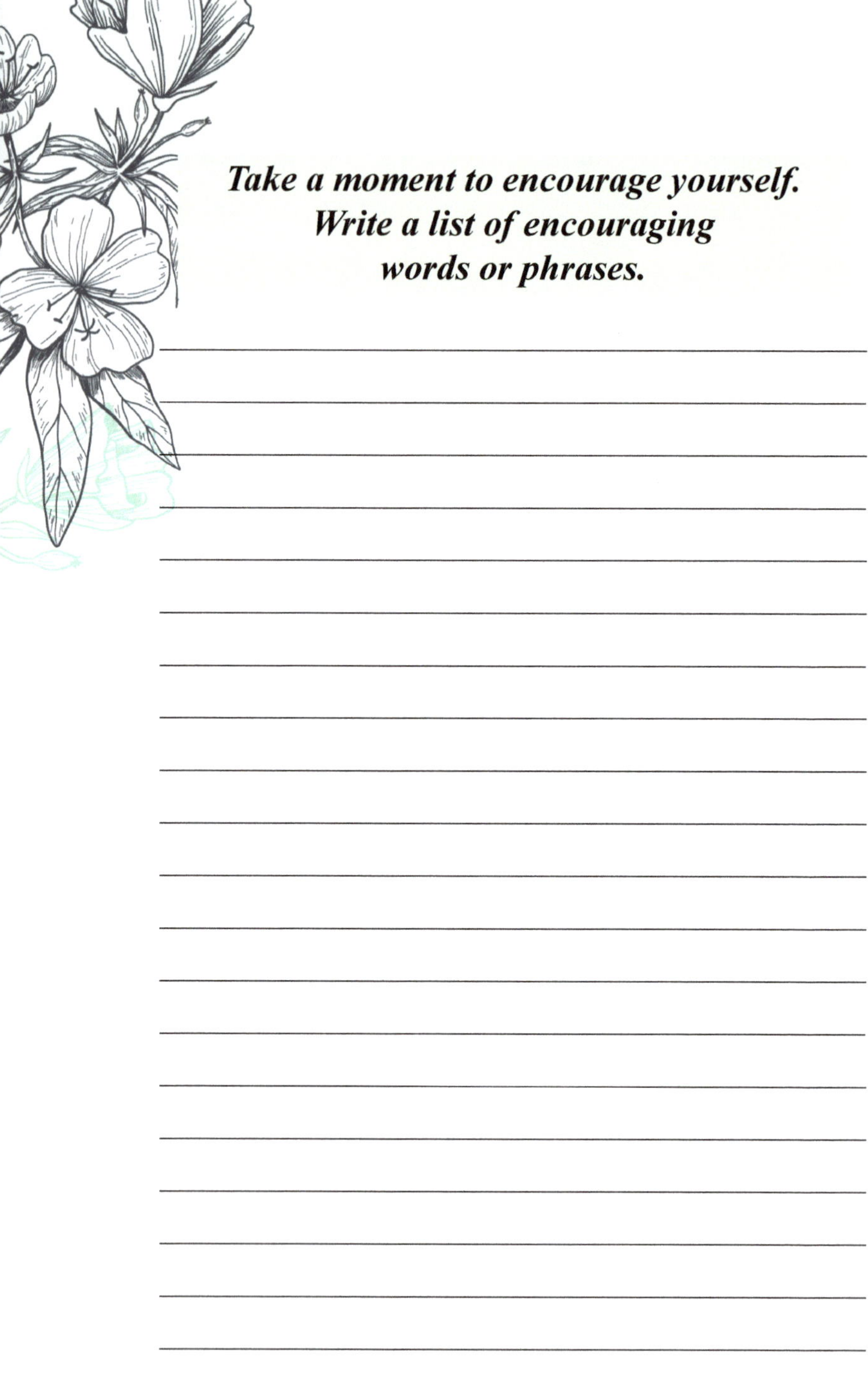

***Take a moment to encourage yourself.
Write a list of encouraging
words or phrases.***

I attract love.
Love flows to and
through me.

Date________________

Morning ○ Afternoon ○ Evening ○

I attract love.
Love flows to and
through me.

Write and repeat todays affirmation three times:

1. ______________________________
2. ______________________________
3. ______________________________

What does this affirmation mean to you?

____

____

____

____

____

____

____

____

____

____

What kind of love are you attracting?

I am the reason
for my happiness.

Date________________

Morning ○ Afternoon ○ Evening ○

I am the reason
for my happiness.

Write and repeat todays affirmation three times:

1. ____________________
2. ____________________
3. ____________________

What does this affirmation mean to you?

How do you make yourself happy? Write down three things that make you happy.

Elevate

"Our elevation must be the result of self-efforts and work of our own hands. No other human power can accomplish it. If we but determine it shall be so, it will be so."

Martin Delany

I pray for it.
I plan for it.
I work for it.
I go get it.

Date ____________________

Morning ○ Afternoon ○ Evening ○

I pray for it. I plan for it.
I work for it. I go get it.

Write and repeat todays affirmation three times:

1. ______________________________
2. ______________________________
3. ______________________________

What does this affirmation mean to you?

____

____

____

____

____

____

____

____

____

____

What are you praying for?
How are you planning for it?

I release those things that no longer serve my highest good. I welcome all things anew.

Date ______________

Morning ○ Afternoon ○ Evening ○

I release those things that no longer serve my highest good. I welcome all things anew.

Write and repeat todays affirmation three times:

1. ______________________________
2. ______________________________
3. ______________________________

What does this affirmation mean to you?

____
____
____
____
____
____
____
____
____
____

What are you releasing?
What are you welcoming?

I am mentally and emotionally equipped for the journey ahead.

Date ____________

Morning ○ Afternoon ○ Evening ○

I am mentally and emotionally equipped for the journey ahead.

Write and repeat todays affirmation three times:

1. ______________________________
2. ______________________________
3. ______________________________

What does this affirmation mean to you?

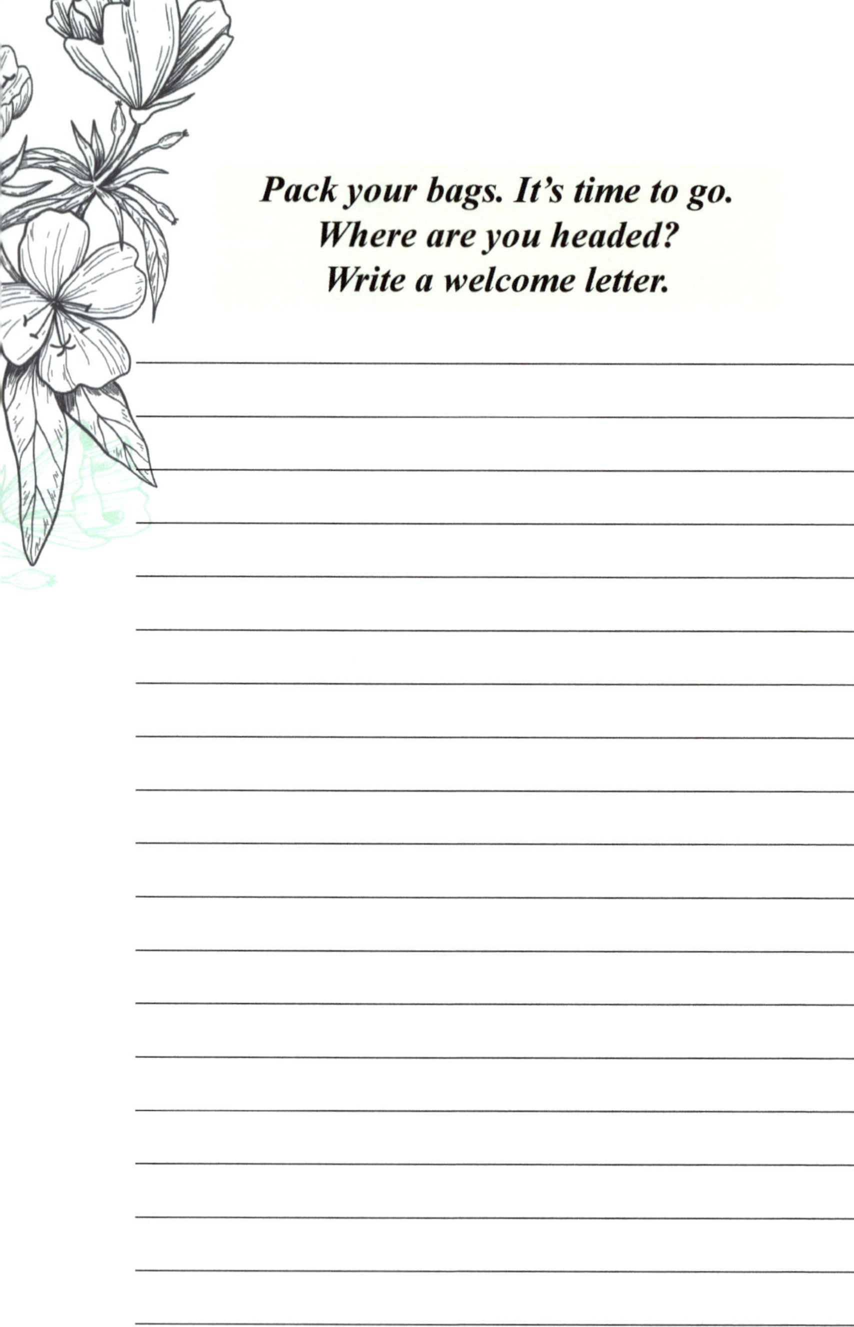

Pack your bags. It's time to go.
Where are you headed?
Write a welcome letter.

I am prepared.
I am equipped.
I am ready for overflow.

Date______________

Morning ○ Afternoon ○ Evening ○

I am prepared. I am equipped.
I am ready for overflow.

Write and repeat todays affirmation three times:

1. ______________________________
2. ______________________________
3. ______________________________

What does this affirmation mean to you?

____
____
____
____
____
____
____
____
____
____

How are you prepared? What do you want to overflow in your life?

My gifts will make room for me.

Date ____________________

Morning ○ Afternoon ○ Evening ○

My gifts will make room for me.

Write and repeat todays affirmation three times:

1. ______________________________________

2. ______________________________________

3. ______________________________________

What does this affirmation mean to you?

____

____

____

____

____

____

____

____

____

____

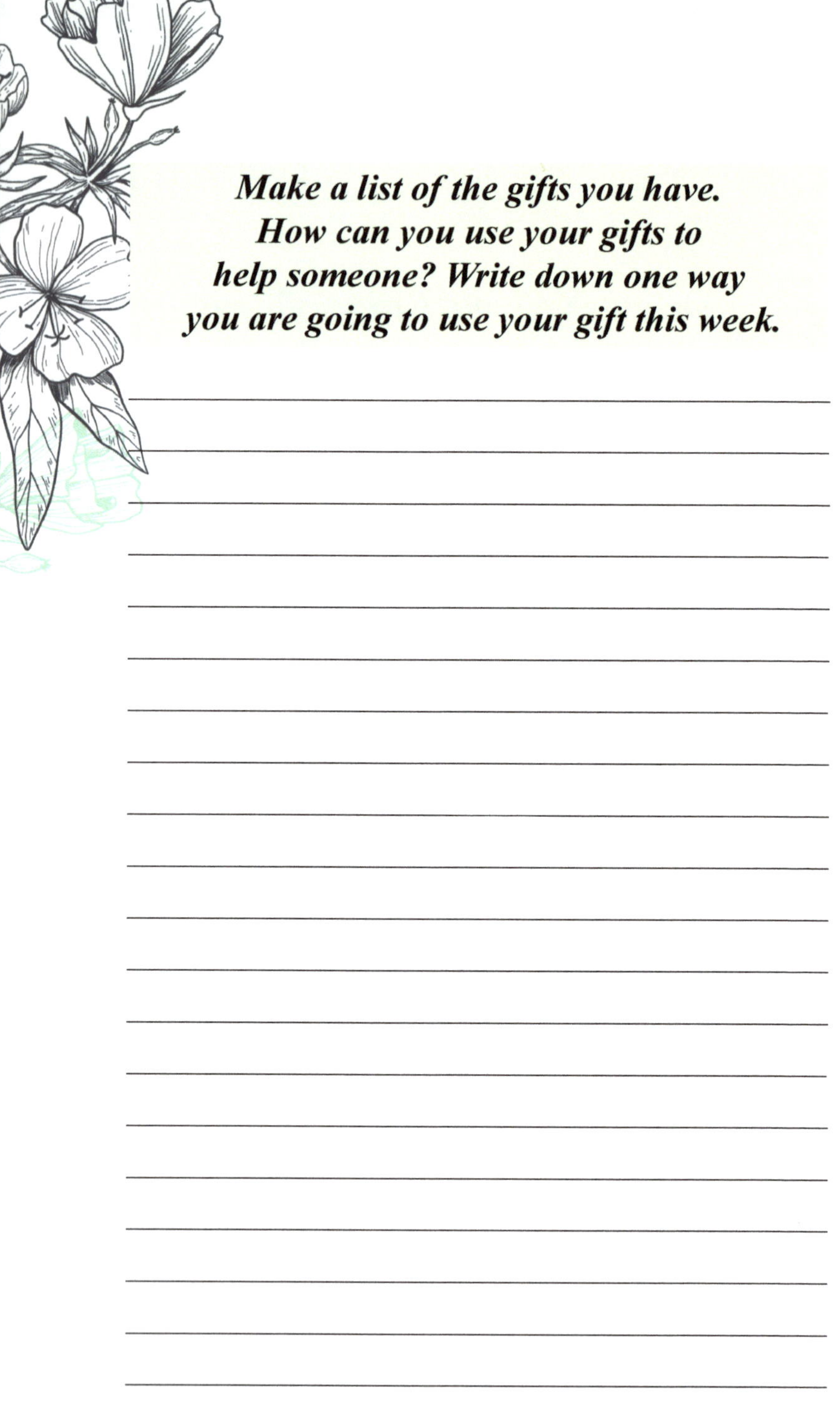

Make a list of the gifts you have. How can you use your gifts to help someone? Write down one way you are going to use your gift this week.

I am the master of
my judgements.
My decisions.
My actions.

Date________________

Morning ○ Afternoon ○ Evening ○

I am the master of my judgements.
My decisions. My actions.

Write and repeat todays affirmation three times:

1. ______________________________
2. ______________________________
3. ______________________________

What does this affirmation mean to you?

____

____

____

____

____

____

____

____

____

____

What is one of the best actions you've taken this week?

I am capable of achieving my financial goals and creating the life I desire.

Date ______________

Morning ○ Afternoon ○ Evening ○

I am capable of achieving my financial goals and creating the life I desire.

Write and repeat todays affirmation three times:

1. ______________________________
2. ______________________________
3. ______________________________

What does this affirmation mean to you?

____

____

____

____

____

____

____

____

____

____

Write down your financial goals? How will your financial goals help you achieve the life you desire?

Affirm

"For there is always light, If only we're brave enough to see it, if only we're brave enough to be it."
Amanda Gorman

I am not anticipating
the next thing.
I am celebrating
the now.

Date ____________________

Morning ○ Afternoon ○ Evening ○

I am not anticipating the next thing.
I am celebrating the now.

Write and repeat todays affirmation three times:

1. ______________________________
2. ______________________________
3. ______________________________

What does this affirmation mean to you?

____

____

____

____

____

____

____

____

____

____

Take a moment to celebrate yourself.
What are you proud of?
P.S. This isn't the time to be shy.

I show gratitude for
where I am.
I show gratitude for
where I will go.

Date ____________

Morning ○ Afternoon ○ Evening ○

I show gratitude for where I am.
I show gratitude for where I will go.

Write and repeat todays affirmation three times:

1. ______________________________
2. ______________________________
3. ______________________________

What does this affirmation mean to you?

____
____
____
____
____
____
____
____
____
____

Take a moment to show gratitude for all you have. Write down 5 things you're grateful for.

I do not define myself
by societies rules.
I make the rules.

Date ____________

Morning ○ Afternoon ○ Evening ○

I do not define myself by societies rules. I make the rules.

Write and repeat todays affirmation three times:

1. ____________
2. ____________
3. ____________

What does this affirmation mean to you?

____

____

____

____

____

____

____

____

____

____

What rules are you making for yourself?
What rules are you neglecting?

I'm in the right place.
At the right time.
With the right people.

Date ____________________

Morning ○ Afternoon ○ Evening ○

I'm in the right place.
At the right time.
With the right people.

Write and repeat todays affirmation three times:

1. ____________________
2. ____________________
3. ____________________

What does this affirmation mean to you?

____
____
____
____
____
____
____
____
____
____

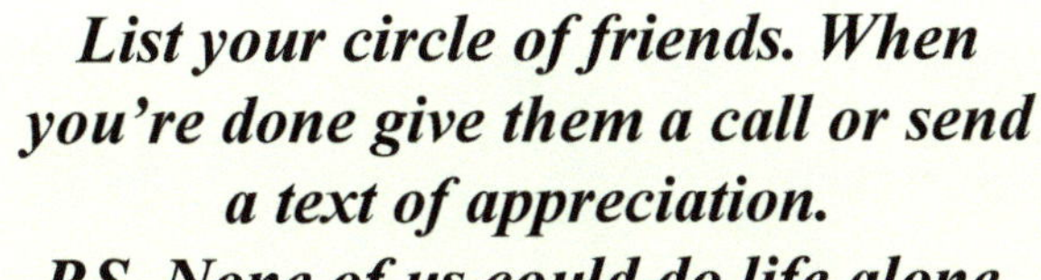

List your circle of friends. When you're done give them a call or send a text of appreciation.

P.S. None of us could do life alone.

I trust myself.
I trust myself to be my best self.

Date ____________

Morning ○ Afternoon ○ Evening ○

I trust myself.
I trust myself to be
my best self.

Write and repeat todays affirmation three times:

1. ____________________________________
2. ____________________________________
3. ____________________________________

What does this affirmation mean to you?

____

____

____

____

____

____

____

____

____

____

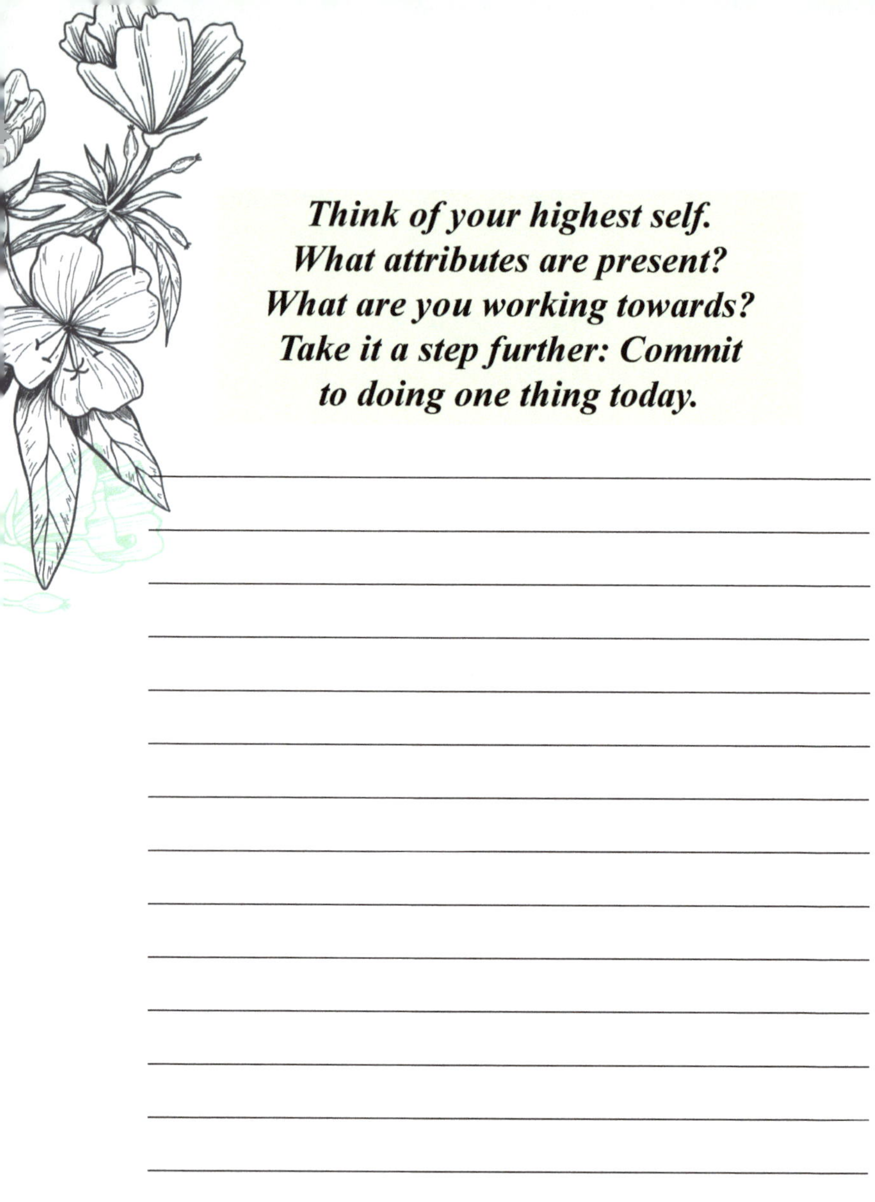

Think of your highest self.
What attributes are present?
What are you working towards?
Take it a step further: Commit
to doing one thing today.

Within myself.
I find myself.

Date________________

Morning ○ Afternoon ○ Evening ○

Within myself.
I find myself.

Write and repeat todays affirmation three times:

1. ____
2. ____
3. ____

What does this affirmation mean to you?

____

____

____

____

____

____

____

____

____

____

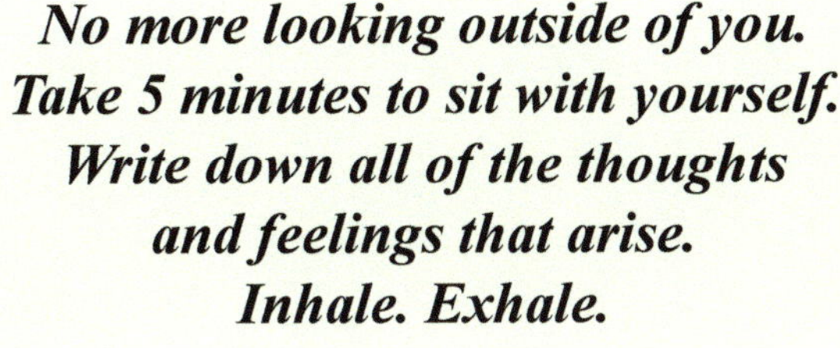

No more looking outside of you.
Take 5 minutes to sit with yourself.
Write down all of the thoughts
and feelings that arise.
Inhale. Exhale.

I am resilient.
I can overcome
challenges.

Date ____________

Morning ○ Afternoon ○ Evening ○

I am resilient.
I can overcome challenges.

Write and repeat todays affirmation three times:

1. ______________________________
2. ______________________________
3. ______________________________

What does this affirmation mean to you?

What challenges have you overcome?
Write down 3 ways you are resilient.
P.S. You are Resilient!

Author Afterword:

I hope these affirmations took you on a journey to your highest self. Evolving is never ending. Engage in these affirmations as often as needed. Cheers to living life on your terms. With gratitude, CR!

Author Bio:

CR is a lover, a sister, a mother, a friend, a life coach! CR is a mother to a beautiful daughter. CR is an avid journaler and believes in the power of affirmations! She holds a bachelors degree from Florida Agriculture and Mechanical University and a Masters degree from John's Hopkins University. CR was an elementary educator for 7 years in both Baltimore and Washington DC! During the day you can find CR working as an instructional designer, at night you can find her providing life coaching services and holding empowering conversations with her clients, and when the dust settles you may find CR with a journal and pen prepping for her next written work of art. For fun CR enjoys spending time with family and friends, nature, and being a mom to her growing little lady!

www.ingramcontent.com/pod-product-compliance
Lightning Source LLC
LaVergne TN
LVHW021336160826
845679LV00008B/1365

9781915930651